# Python Programming Basics

## For Data Science

By Javier Alfredo Candiotti

# Preface

## Simplifying Python Basic Concepts

In my learning journey, I have discovered that simplicity is key to understanding new concepts in Python Programming. By simplifying these concepts, I can learn faster and retain the information better. Therefore, I am summarizing all the concepts I have learned from various sources, including classes and extensive data from the internet. Additionally, I am disclosing that I have used Artificial Intelligence to assist in writing this book, specifically ChatGPT.

The purpose of this book is to educate and guide new students or anyone interested in Data Science to learn the basic concepts of Python Programming in the simplest way possible. **My personal goal is to accelerate the Singularity as much as we can, using AGI, so we can solve all the health, environmental, and economic problems of the world and finally concentrate on deep space exploration.**
I hope this book serves as a helpful guide in your learning journey.

Best of luck and wishing you only the best in your learning endeavors!

Javier Alfredo Candiotti
April 17, 2023
CA, USA

# Contents

# Chapter 1

# Basic Python Programming Concepts

Python is a popular and widely used programming language in data science due to its simplicity, readability, and flexibility.

Here are some basic Python Programming Concepts that are important for data science.

## 1.1 Variables and data types

In Python, variables are used to store data. There are several data types in Python, such as integer, float, string, Boolean, and more. To create a variable you simply need to assign a value using the equal sign (=). Example:

```
x = 5
y = "Hello, World!"
z = 3.36769
```

## 1.2 List and Arrays

Lists are a way to store multiple values in one variable. Arrays are similar to lists but they are used specifically for numerical data. Example:

```
my_list = [1, 2, 3, 4, 5]
```

## 1.3 Control flow statements

Control flow statements are used to control the flow of execution in a program. Examples are if-else statements, while loops, and for loops. Here's an example of an if-else statement:

```
x = 10
if x > 5:
    print("x is greater than 5")
else:
    print("x is less than or equal to 5")
```

## 1.4 Functions

Functions are reusable blocks of code that perform specific tasks. They can take inputs and return outputs. Example:

```
def square(x):
    return x * x
```

## 1.5 Libraries and Modules

Python has many libraries and modules that extend its functionality. Some commonly used libraries are NumPy, Pandas, and Matplotlib. Here's an example of importing the NumPy library:

```
import numpy as np
```

These are a few basic concepts in Python Programming that are important for Data Science. We will go into more detail in the following pages. Note that in the examples of codes, everything after '#' is just a comment on what the code does.

Python does not read anything after '#'; programmers write them to remember what that code does. Comments are helpful in remembering the function of a specific code, especially for programs that have hundreds or thousands of lines of code, and also for anyone else who may read the code.

# Chapter 2

# Variables and Data Types

## 2.1 Variables

Variables are used to store data in a program. A variable is like a container that holds a value, which can be changed or updated during the execution of a program. In Python, you can create a variable by assigning a value to it using the assignment operator (=). Notice that in Python, the equal sign does not mean equality like in mathematics.

For example, to create a variable named "x" and assign it the value of 7, you can write:

```
x = 7
```

In Python, variables can store different types of data, such as integers, floating-point numbers, strings, and more. The type of data a variable can store is determined by the type of value assigned to it.

## 2.2 Data Types

In Python, there are several built-in data types that you can use to store different kinds of data. Some of the most common data types in Python are

- Integer: A whole number, such as 1, 2, 3, and so on.
- Float: A number with a decimal point, such as 3.14, 2.5, and so on.
- Boolean: A data type that can have only two values: True or False.
- String: A sequence of characters enclosed in quotes, such as "hello", "world", and so on.
- List: A collection of values that can be of different data types, enclosed in square brackets, such as [1, 2, 3], ["hello", "world"], and so on.
- Tuple: A collection of values that can be of different data types, enclosed in parentheses, such as (1, 2, 3), ("hello", "world"), and so on.
- Dictionary: A collection of key-value pairs, enclosed in curly braces, such as {"name": "John", "age": 33}, {"name": "Mary", "age": 25}, and so on.

## 2.3 Integers

An integer is a whole number, it doesn't have a decimal point. In Python, you can create an integer variable by assigning a whole number to it. For example, to create an integer variable named "age" and assign it the value of 25, you can write:

```
age = 25
```

You can perform various operations on integers, such as addition (+), subtraction (-), multiplication (*), division (/), and more. For example:

```
x = 5
y = 3
z = x + y # z will be 8
w = x * y # w will be 15
q = x / y # q will be 1.6666666666666667
```

In Python, you can also use the modulo operator (%) to get the remainder of a division operation. For example:

```
x = 5
y = 3
z = x % y # z will be 2
```

## 2.4 Floats

A float is a number with a decimal point. In Python, you can create a float variable by assigning a number with a decimal point to it. For example:

```
pi = 3.14
```

You can perform various operations on floats, such as addition (+), subtraction (-), multiplication (*), division (/), and more. For example:

```
x = 3.14
y = 2.5
z = x + y # z will be 5.64
w = x * y # w will be 7.85
```

## 2.5 Booleans

A boolean is a data type or result that can have only two values: True or False. In Python, you can create a boolean variable by assigning either True or False to it. For example:

```
is_raining = True
```

You can use boolean variables in conditional statements, such as if-else statements and while loops. For example:

```
is_raining = True

if is_raining:
    print("Bring an umbrella")
else:
    print("No need for an umbrella")
```

This code will print "Bring an umbrella" since the value of the is_raining variable is True.

## 2.6 Strings

A string is a sequence of characters enclosed in quotes. In Python, you can create a string variable by enclosing a sequence of characters in either single quotes (') or double quotes (""). For example:

```
name = "John"
message = 'Hello, world!'
```

You can perform various operations on strings, such as concatenation (+), repetition (*), and indexing ([]). For example:

```
first_name = "John"
last_name = "Doe"
full_name = first_name + " " + last_name # full_name will be "John Doe"

greeting = "Hello, " * 3 # greeting will be "Hello, Hello, Hello, "

first_letter = name[0] # first_letter will be "J"
```

## 2.7 Lists

A list is a collection of values that can be of different data types, enclosed in square brackets. In Python, you can create a list variable by enclosing a sequence of values in square brackets, separated by commas. For example:

```
numbers = [1, 2, 3, 4, 5]
fruits = ["apple", "banana", "orange"]
```

You can perform various operations on lists, such as indexing ([]), slicing ([:]), appending (append()), and more. For example:

```
first_number = numbers[0] # first_number will be 1
```

```
first_two_numbers = numbers[:2] # first_two_numbers will be [1, 2]
```

```
numbers.append(6) # numbers will be [1, 2, 3, 4, 5, 6]
```

## 2.8 Tuples

A tuple is a collection of values that can be of different data types, enclosed in parentheses. In Python, you can create a tuple variable by enclosing a sequence of values in parentheses, separated by commas. For example:

```
person = ("John", 30, "male")
```

You can perform various operations on tuples, such as indexing ([ ]), slicing ([:]), and more. However, you cannot modify the values of a tuple once it is created, unlike a list.

## 2.9 Dictionaries

A dictionary is a collection of key-value pairs, enclosed in curly braces. In Python, you can create a dictionary variable by enclosing a sequence of key-value pairs in curly braces, separated by commas. For example:

```
person = {"name": "John", "age": 30, "gender": "male"}
```

You can access the values of a dictionary by using the keys, like this:

```
name = person["name"] # name will be "John"
```

You can also modify the values of a dictionary by using the keys, like this:

```
person["age"] = 31 # the age of the person will be updated to 31
```

In this chapter, we have covered the basics of variables and data types in Python programming. Understanding these concepts is essential for data science, as they are used to store and manipulate data in a program. By mastering these concepts, you can start writing Python programs for data analysis and machine learning. Also, as soon as you learn the basics of Python programming, you will be able to learn any other programming language much easier.

# Chapter 3

# Lists and Arrays in Python

Lists and arrays are two of the most commonly used data structures in Python programming. They allow you to store and manipulate collections of values, which can be of different data types, such as integers, floats, strings, etc. In this chapter, we will explore the basics of lists and arrays in Python, including how to create and manipulate them, and their applications in data science.

## 3.1 Lists in Python

A list is a collection of values that can be of different data types, enclosed in square brackets [ ]. In Python, you can create a list by enclosing a sequence of values in square brackets, separated by commas. For example:

```
my_list = [1, 2, 3, "four", 5.0]
```

Here, my_list is a list that contains five values:

an integer 1, an integer 2, an integer 3, a string "four", and a float 5.0. You can access the values in a list by using indexing, which starts from 0. For example:

```
print(my_list[0])   # Output: 1
print(my_list[3])   # Output: "four"
```

You can also modify the values in a list by using indexing. For example:

```
my_list[4] = 6.0
print(my_list)   # Output: [1, 2, 3, "four", 6.0]
```

In addition to indexing, lists support a range of operations, such as slicing, appending, and sorting. For example:

11

```
# Slicing a list
print(my_list[1:3])   # Output: [2, 3]

# Appending to a list
my_list.append(7)
print(my_list)   # Output: [1, 2, 3, "four", 6.0, 7]

# Sorting a list
my_list.sort()
print(my_list)   # Output: [1, 2, 3, 6.0, 7, "four"]
```

## 3.2 Arrays in Python

An array is a collection of values of the same data type, stored in contiguous memory locations. Unlike lists, arrays are more efficient in terms of memory and performance, especially when dealing with large datasets. In Python, you can create an array using the array module, which provides a way to create and manipulate arrays. For example:

```
import array as arr

my_array = arr.array("i", [1, 2, 3, 4, 5])
```

Here, my_array is an array of integers, which contains five values: 1, 2, 3, 4, and 5. The first argument to the array function specifies the type of the array, which can be one of the following: b (signed char), B (unsigned char), h (short), H (unsigned short), i (int), I (unsigned int), l (long), L (unsigned long), f (float), or d (double).

You can access the values in an array by using indexing, similar to lists. For example:

```
print(my_array[0])   # Output: 1
print(my_array[3])   # Output: 4
```

You can also modify the values in an array by using indexing. For example:

```
my_array[4] = 6
print(my_array)   # Output: array('i', [1,2,3,4,6])
```

Now the number 4 has become number 6.

# Chapter 4

# Control Flow Statements

Control flow statements in Python are used to control the flow of program execution. They allow you to execute certain code blocks based on specific conditions or repeat code blocks a certain number of times.

There are three main types of control flow statements in Python: if/else statements, loops, and function calls.

## 4.1 If/Else Statements

If/else statements are used to execute a code block if a condition is true or execute a different code block if the condition is false. Here's an example:

```
x = 10

if x > 5:
    print("x is greater than 5")
else:
    print("x is less than or equal to 5")
```

In this example, the condition x > 5 is true, so the code block under the if statement is executed, which prints "x is greater than 5". If the condition were false, the code block under the else statement would be executed instead.

## 4.2 Loops

Loops are used to repeat code blocks a certain number of times or until a certain condition is met. There are two main types of loops in Python: 'for' loops and 'while' loops.

A 'for' loop is used to iterate over a sequence, such as a list or a string. Here's an example:

```
fruits = ["apple", "banana", "cherry"]

for fruit in fruits:
    print(fruit)
```

In this example, the 'for' loop iterates over the 'fruits' list and prints each element.

A 'while' loop is used to repeat a code block until a certain condition is met. Here's an example:

```
x = 0

while x < 5:
    print(x)
    x += 1
```

In this example, the 'while' loop repeats the code block under it as long as the condition x < 5 is true. It starts with x = 0 and prints the value of 'x' on each iteration until 'x' is incremented to 5 and the condition is no longer true.

## 4.3 Function Calls

Function calls are used to execute a specific block of code, which can be reused multiple times throughout your program. Here's an example:

```
def greet(name):
    print("Hello, " + name + "!")

greet("Alice")
greet("Bob")
```

In this example, the 'greet' function takes a name argument and prints a greeting message using the value of 'name'. The function is called twice with different arguments, printing "Hello, Alice!" and "Hello, Bob!".

That's a summarized overview of control flow statements in Python. I hope that helps!

# Chapter 5

# Functions

Functions allow you to encapsulate a block of code that performs a specific task and reuse it multiple times throughout your program. This not only makes your code more modular and easier to read, but it also saves you time and effort by eliminating the need to rewrite the same code over and over again.

In Python, you define a function using the 'def' keyword, followed by the function name and any arguments that the function takes. The code block under the 'def' statement is called the function body, and it contains the instructions that the function executes when it is called.

## 5.1 Simple Functions

Here is an example of a simple function that takes two arguments and returns their sum:

```
def add_numbers(x, y):
    sum = x + y
    return sum
```

In this example, the function 'add_numbers' takes two arguments, 'x' and 'y', and calculates their sum using the '+' operator. The result is stored in the 'sum' variable, which is then returned using the 'return' keyword.

## 5.2 Call a Function

To call a function in Python, you simply write its name followed by any arguments that it takes, enclosed in parentheses. Here's how you would call the 'add_numbers' function from above:

```
result = add_numbers(5, 7)
print(result)   # Output: 12
```

In this example, we pass the values '5' and '7' as arguments to the 'add_numbers' function, and it returns their sum, which is stored in the 'result' variable. We then print the value of 'result', which is 12.

## 5.3 Functions with Default Argument Values

Functions can also have default argument values, which are used if the function is called without providing a value for that argument. Here's an example:

```python
def greet(name, greeting="Hello"):
    print(greeting + ", " + name + "!")

greet("Alice")            # Output: Hello, Alice!
greet("Bob", "Hi there")   # Output: Hi there, Bob!
```

In this example, the 'greet' function takes two arguments, 'name' and 'greeting'. If the 'greeting' argument is not provided when the function is called, it defaults to "Hello". The function then prints a greeting message using the provided or default values.

## 5.4 Functions using Tuples

Functions can also return multiple values using tuples. Here's an example:

```python
def calculate(x, y):
    sum = x + y
    difference = x - y
    product = x * y
    quotient = x / y
    return sum, difference, product, quotient

result = calculate(10, 5)
print(result)   # Output: (15, 5, 50, 2.0)
```

In this example, the 'calculate' function takes two arguments, 'x' and 'y', and calculates their sum, difference, product, and quotient. The values are returned as a tuple, which is then stored in the 'result' variable and printed.

Functions can also take an arbitrary number of arguments using the '*arg's and '**kwargs' syntax. Here's an example:

```
def print_args(*args, **kwargs):
    print("Positional arguments:")
    for arg in args:
        print(arg)
    print("Keyword arguments:")
    for key, value in kwargs.items():
        print(key + " = " + str(value))

print_args(1, "hello", True, name="Alice", age=30)

# Output
Positional arguments:
1
hello
True
Keyword arguments:
name = Alice
age = 30
```

In this example, 'the print_args' function takes an arbitrary number of positional arguments using the '*args' syntax, and an arbitrary number of keyword arguments using the '**kwargs' syntax. The function then prints each argument in the args tuple and each key-value pair in the 'kwargs' dictionary.

## 5.5 Functions inside Functions

Functions can also be defined inside other functions and can be returned as values from other functions. These are known as nested functions and higher-order functions, respectively. Here's an example:

```
def outer_function(x):
    def inner_function(y):
        return y * 2
    return inner_function(x)

result = outer_function(5)
print(result)  # Output: 10
```

In this example, 'the outer_function' takes an argument 'x' and defines a nested function 'inner_function' that takes an argument 'y' and returns 'y * 2'. The outer_function then returns the result of calling 'inner_function' with the 'x' argument. The value '10' is stored in the 'result' variable and printed.

Finally, functions can also be used as arguments to other functions, which is known as a callback function. Here's an example:

```python
def square(x):
    return x ** 2

def apply(func, x):
    return func(x)

result = apply(square, 5)
print(result)   # Output: 25
```

In this example, the 'square' function takes an argument 'x' and returns its square. The 'apply' function takes a function 'func' and an argument 'x', and applies the function to the argument. The value '25' is stored in the 'result' variable and printed.

In conclusion, functions are a fundamental building block of Python programming and are essential for writing reusable, modular, and efficient code. By encapsulating blocks of code into functions, you can avoid repetitive code, improve code readability, and facilitate code maintenance.

# Chapter 6

# Libraries and Modules

Python is a powerful programming language with a vast collection of built-in functions and data types that can be used to create complex applications. However, to take full advantage of the language, you may need to use external libraries and modules that provide additional functionality and features beyond what is included in the Python standard library.

In this introduction, we'll explore the concepts of libraries and modules in Python, and how they can be used to extend the language's capabilities.

## 6.1 What are libraries and modules?

In Python, a library is a collection of modules that provide specific functionality for a particular task or domain. A module is a file containing Python code that defines functions, classes, and variables that can be imported and used in other Python code.

Libraries and modules can be installed using the pip package manager or included as part of a Python distribution. Some popular Python libraries include NumPy for numerical computing, pandas for data analysis, and Matplotlib for data visualization.

## 6.2 Importing Modules

To use a module in your Python code, you first need to import it. You can import a module using the import keyword, followed by the name of the module. For example, to import the math module, you can use the following code:

```python
import math
```

Once you've imported a module, you can access its contents using dot notation. For example, to use the 'sqrt' function from the 'math' module to calculate the square root of a number, you can use the following code:

```python
import math

x = 16
y = math.sqrt(x)

print(y)   # Output: 4.0
```

## 6.3 Aliasing modules

If you want to use a shorter or more convenient name for a module in your code, you can use the 'as' keyword to alias the module name. For example, to import the 'pandas' module and use the alias 'pd', you can use the following code:

```
import pandas as pd
```

Once you've aliased a module, you can use the alias instead of the full module name to access its contents. For example, to use the 'DataFrame' class from the 'pandas' module, you can use the following code:

```
import pandas as pd

data = {'name': ['Alice', 'Bob', 'Charlie'], 'age': [25, 30, 35]}
df = pd.DataFrame(data)

print(df)

# Output:

    name  age
0   Alice  25
1    Bob   30
2 Charlie  35
```

## 6.4 Importing Specific Items from Modules

If you only need to use specific functions, classes, or variables from a module, you can import them directly using the 'from' keyword, followed by the module name and the item name. For example, to import only the 'sqrt' function from the math module, you can use the following code:

```
from math import sqrt

x = 16
y = sqrt(x)

print(y)   # Output: 4.0
```

Once you've imported specific items from a module, you can use them directly in your code without the module prefix.

## 6.5 Creating your own Modules

In addition to using existing Python modules, you can also create your own modules to organize your code into reusable and modular components. To create a module, you simply need to define a Python file containing the code you want to reuse and save it with a '.py' extension in a directory that is included in the Python module search path.

For example, suppose you have a file named 'my_module.py' containing the following code:

```
def add(x, y):
    return x + y

def subtract(x, y):
```

Once you've defined a module, you can import it into your Python code using the 'import' statement. For example, suppose you have a file named 'my_script.py' that uses the functions defined in 'my_module.py'. To use these functions in 'my_script.py', you can import the module using the following code:

```
import my_module

x = 5
y = 10

result = my_module.add(x, y)

print(result)   # Output: 15
```

In this example, we first import the 'my_module' module using the 'import' statement. We can then use the 'add' function from the 'my_module' module to add the values of 'x' and 'y'.

You can also use the 'from' keyword to import specific functions or variables from a module. For example, to import only the 'add' function from the 'my_module' module, you can use the following code:

```
from my_module import add

x = 5
y = 10

result = add(x, y)

print(result)   # Output: 15
```

In this example, we only import the 'add' function from the 'my_module' module using the from keyword. We can then use the 'add' function directly in our code without the module prefix.

## 6.6 Using external libraries

In addition to using Python's built-in modules and your own custom modules, you can also use external libraries and modules to extend the functionality of Python. External libraries and modules are typically distributed as packages, which can be installed using the pip package manager.
To install a package using pip, you can use the following command:

```
pip install package_name
```

Once you've installed a package, you can import it into your Python code using the 'import' statement, just like you would with a built-in module or a custom module.
For example, to use the 'numpy' library for numerical computing, you can install it using the following command:

```
pip install numpy
```

You can then import the numpy library into your Python code using the following code:

```
import numpy as np

x = np.array([1, 2, 3])
y = np.array([4, 5, 6])

result = np.dot(x, y)

print(result)   # Output: 32
```

In this example, we first import the 'numpy' library using the 'import' statement, and alias it as 'np'. We can then use the 'np.array' function to create arrays, and the 'np.dot' function to calculate the dot product of the arrays.

In summary, libraries and modules are essential components of Python programming that allow you to extend the language's functionality beyond its built-in capabilities. By learning how to import and use modules, as well as how to create your own modules, you can write more modular and reusable code that can be easily maintained and scaled. Additionally, by leveraging external libraries and packages, you can access a vast collection of tools and resources that can help you solve complex problems in fields such as data science, machine learning, and web development.

# Chapter 7

# Additional Programming Languages

Data science is an interdisciplinary field that combines statistical analysis, machine learning, and computer science to extract insights and knowledge from data. While Python is widely considered the dominant language for data science due to its ease of use, a vast collection of libraries and tools, and strong community support, there are several other programming languages that can be useful for data scientists to learn. In this chapter, we will explore three programming languages that are commonly used in data science: R, SQL, and Julia.

## 7.1 R

R is a programming language and environment for statistical computing and graphics. It is widely used in data analysis, machine learning, and scientific research, and has a large collection of libraries and packages specifically designed for statistical analysis. R's syntax is similar to that of Python, making it relatively easy for Python users to learn. However, R's focus on statistical analysis sets it apart from Python, which is a more general-purpose language.

Some of the key features of R include:

- Built-in support for statistical analysis, including linear regression, time series analysis, and clustering.
- A large collection of libraries and packages for data manipulation, visualization, and machine learning.
- Interactive data visualization tools that allow users to create custom plots and charts.
- Integrated development environments (IDEs) such as RStudio that provide a user-friendly interface for data analysis.
- Learning R can be beneficial for data scientists who work with large datasets or need to perform complex statistical analyses. R's focus on statistics and its extensive library of packages make it a powerful tool for data analysis and modeling.

## 7.2 SQL

SQL (Structured Query Language) is a programming language used to manage and manipulate relational databases. While SQL is not a general-purpose programming language like Python or R, it is an essential tool for data scientists who work with large datasets stored in databases. SQL is used to perform a wide range of tasks, including querying, updating, and managing data.

Some of the key features of SQL include:

- Ability to manipulate and query large datasets stored in databases.
- Support for data analysis through functions and operators.
- Easy integration with other programming languages, including Python and R.
- Learning SQL can be useful for data scientists who need to work with large, complex datasets stored in databases. SQL is a powerful tool for managing and querying data, and its integration with other programming languages makes it a valuable addition to a data scientist's skillset.

## 7.3 Julia

Julia is a high-level, high-performance programming language designed for scientific computing, numerical analysis, and data science. Julia is known for its speed, flexibility, and ease of use, making it a popular choice for data scientists who need to perform computationally intensive tasks. Julia's syntax is similar to that of MATLAB and Python, making it relatively easy to learn.

Some of the key features of Julia include:

- High-performance computing capabilities that allow users to perform complex computations quickly.
- Built-in support for distributed computing, allowing users to run computations on multiple machines.
- A large collection of libraries and packages for data manipulation, visualization, and machine learning.
- Learning Julia can be beneficial for data scientists who need to perform computationally intensive tasks, such as numerical simulations or optimization problems. Julia's high-performance computing capabilities and support for distributed computing make it a powerful tool for data science.

## 7.4 Conclusion

In conclusion, while Python is the dominant language for data science, there are several other programming languages that can be useful for data scientists to learn. R, SQL, and Julia are three such languages that are commonly used in data science. R's focus on statistical analysis and its extensive library of packages make it a powerful tool for data analysis and modeling. SQL is an essential tool for managing and querying large datasets stored in databases. Julia's high-performance computing capabilities make it a valuable tool for performing computationally intensive tasks. By learning these languages, data scientists can expand their skillset and become more versatile in their work. Additionally, learning multiple programming languages can also provide a deeper understanding of programming concepts and increase problem-solving abilities.

It is important to note that while learning these languages can be beneficial, it is not necessary to master all of them. The choice of which language to learn depends on the specific needs of the data scientist and the tasks they need to perform. For example, a data scientist working with large, complex datasets stored in databases would benefit more from learning SQL, while a data scientist working on computationally intensive tasks may find Julia more useful.

In addition to these three languages, there are several other languages that may be useful for data scientists to learn, depending on their specific needs. For example, MATLAB is commonly used in scientific research and engineering, while Scala is used for big data processing. However, it is important to prioritize learning the most widely used and popular languages before moving on to more niche languages.

In conclusion, while Python is the dominant language for data science, learning other programming languages can be beneficial for data scientists to expand their skillset and become more versatile in their work. R, SQL, and Julia are three commonly used languages in data science that provide specific advantages in statistical analysis, database management, and high-performance computing, respectively. By learning these languages, data scientists can improve their ability to solve complex problems and extract insights from data.